Adventures in a Ford Model T:
The Making of a T-raveler

———●———

By Jason Bogstie

Cover photo courtesy of John Laughlin

First Edition, 2025

eBook edition first published in 2025

Paperback edition first published in 2025

ISBN 979-8-9985886-0-0 (EPUB eBook)

ISBN 979-8-9985886-1-7 (Paperback)

Library of Congress Control Number: 2025906875

Self-published in Cheyenne, Wyoming

www.JasonBogstie.com

Dedicated to the Seekers and the Wonderers.

"Like I always say, pull those ears down and let her go!" – Red Runkle, 1983 President Model T Ford Club of America

JusT Another Day

It was a sunny and beautiful August day when the Curse of Pine Bluffs snuck up on me. The top on my 1919 Model T Touring was down, warm wind in my face and my right arm was outstretched across the front seat. I was hosting this tour and being the lead vehicle was making it a banner day. I glanced in my rearview mirror and saw the convoy - an assortment of nine other Model Ts following behind me. I was less than one mile from the city limits, almost there! As I approached an unsignaled railroad crossing at 35 miles per hour, I glanced quickly to my left and right to make sure no trains were coming and proceeded to cross. My car popped over the railroad tracks as I immediately heard the unnerving and atypical sound of steel and asphalt grinding against each other in an angry fashion. I immediately attempted to pull over and was bewildered that my steering was gone. I stepped on the brakes and discovered that those, too, were not stopping me. In a panic, I pulled firmly on the handbrake to my left. Much to my relief, I began to slow down and veer to the side of the road. What felt like minutes, was in reality seconds. I was 200 feet from the railroad crossing. Wondering what happened, I sat up and looked behind me. I was flabbergasted! The Curse of Pine Bluffs struck again! This time the curse may have ended my journeys once and for all...

I hate travelling. That's funny to say coming from someone who owns and drives a 1919 Ford Model T on a somewhat regular basis. It's not the destinations I dislike so much as it is the hustle and bustle of modern travel. I live in Wyoming. Travel options to many places are limited. The easiest option, while being the most logistically complicated option, is flying. In order to make the day more efficient, my flights are always at the crack of dawn, meaning I have to be up and ready to go not long after the midnight oil has run out. I hustle my bags into my modern car, drive at breakneck speeds on modern roads, fueled by caffeine (God willing) and sheer adrenaline, just to arrive at a parking lot many miles from the airport. After unloading my bags, I rush to get on a shuttle that drives me to the terminal where I have to deal with a crowd of people, sleepy airline staff and the ever so joyful folks at the TSA. Sure, many of them are polite and friendly, but it seems to me that just as many are not. More often than not, something about my person sets off an alarm and off to secondary screening I go. I remember one time the body scanner showed some "anomaly" directly over my crotch. I was not carrying anything other than modest body anatomy, but it resulted in a secondary screening bordering on an assault; something that would certainly get me fired if I were to do the same to someone at my place of work. Then it's off to the terminal, where I wait...and wait...oops the flight was delayed...wait some more. On and on until finally I get the privilege of being crammed into a tin can, a flying brick, where I will likely catch some cold while eating a small snack included with my many hundreds of dollars plane ticket. Then the plane lands and it's time to figure out where my bags are and find some ground transportation to my destination. Exhausting!!

The only other viable option for someone living where I do, in Wyoming, is to drive. Modern cars are much more comfortable to ride in than cars such as my Model T. Sound proofing and insulation, adjustable heat and air conditioning, and a radio all make driving a car a peaceful and disconnected endeavor. One problem I suffer from, according to my wife, is *carcolepsy*. For whatever reason I have never figured out, even if I am driving, after a number of minutes of highway speeds I start to get drowsy. It has gotten worse as I have gotten older. I find my best option is to chew some gum, or eat something to keep from getting too drowsy, but sometimes that does not work.

Sometimes, nothing helps; not singing along to the radio, not windows down at 75 miles per hour, nothing! I try to encourage my wife to drive when we have someplace to go that's not immediately in town so as to not have to deal with this issue. When I am on my own, I find myself stopping at rest areas just to walk around the car once or twice or pulling off to shut my eyes for a few minutes.

The Union Pacific Railroad passes right through Cheyenne and has a full-sized maintenance yard. I would personally love to take a train but sadly, the UP line only handles freight. There is no passenger service. If I lived closer to Denver, I could get on an Amtrak train and get around to some of the farther off places I need to go. Traffic into Denver from Cheyenne is terrible plus I'd have to stay awake for the 2.5-hour drive south from Cheyenne.

This is where the Ford Model T comes in. Driving one of these contraptions is not a disconnected or passive experience by any means. You have control over the speed and engine timing. Your muscles have control over a powerless steering system. You travel between 30 - 40 miles per hour with brakes that are controlled by engine-assisted braking, by stock. Driving a Model T puts you in control of the driving experience as much as a car can. Maybe that's partly why I don't suffer from 'carcolepsy' when I am driving my Model T. Perhaps it's also the smells and sounds connecting me from my modern-day drive, all the way back in time to whomever first owned my car in 1919. That's a lot of history to be driving around in. That's 106 years of history at the time of this writing! I don't know how someone can sleep when physically manipulating the controls of something that has seen so many revolutions around the sun. After a while, you find a direct connection to that much history changes you.

Infected with a different kind of 'T-Cell'

I had never known about the Model T until I launched my career. In 2012, I graduated from the University of Wyoming with a master's degree in Anthropology. My focus was archaeology. Figuring out human history through humanity's trash was my chosen career path. The problem with that career path is always finding gainful employment that doesn't require living out of a hotel or competing for a tenure-track position at a university. After some struggling and getting laid off from a job I was hoping would pan-out long term, I got hired by the Wyoming Department of Transportation (WYDOT). In November 2013, I became their Senior Cultural Resources Specialist. I was hired to help WYDOT stay in compliance with Federal historic preservation laws. It was a huge career break for me. At the time, I did not realize how much transportation would end up being such a big part of my life. The impacts were not only professionally meaningful, but the historical associations resulted in deep impacts to my personal life as well.

Wyoming has something in the neighborhood of 28,326 miles of official roads. Three interstate highways cross Wyoming, totaling 914 miles. There are around 2,796 public vehicular bridges statewide. That's a lot of driving! While the Interstate Highway is now historically significant, there are other historic major roads in Wyoming (I say major because there are many smaller, local roads that allowed for the development of different pockets of Wyoming). These roads include the Old Yellowstone Highway, National Park to Park Highway, Rocky Mountain Highway, Black and Yellow Trail, and others I am sure I am forgetting. Despite all of the historic roads I became familiar with while working at WYDOT, it was the first transcontinental road, which happened to pass right through Wyoming, that captured my attention personally and professionally and the one that ultimately infected me with T-Cells of a different kind. The Lincoln Highway.

The Lincoln Highway was the successful result of the Good Roads Movement. Ironically, the Good Roads Movement was started in the 1890s by bicyclists who wanted something better on which to ride. Prior to modern roads, there were no good ways to get around. Paths existed to get around on ranches, and dirty interconnected mud wallows pockmarked the way through towns. There was really nothing to get from town to town and all of these paths that existed were of extremely poor quality. The League of American Wheelmen were resourceful in their approach. The arguments they made were focused largely to farmers emphasizing the importance good roads would have in getting their crops to market. Slow and steady, like a Model T, this movement began picking up momentum. Eventually, the movement got the attention of the early automobile pioneers. Carl Fisher, an entrepreneur from Indiana, had a dream of a road that crossed the entire country. He succeeded in motivating some of his friends to help finance his transcontinental dream, and after naming the road after Fisher's hero, Abraham Lincoln, the Lincoln Highway Association was founded to get the road built.

The Lincoln Highway starts at Times Square, New York (the Eastern Terminus) and crosses 14 states, ending in Lincoln Park, San Francisco (the Western Terminus). The road started out as a connection of the many local town roads and the repurpose of abandoned railroad grades. Over its existence the Lincoln Highway was continually improved, and the alignment of the road was refined to make the path more efficient and eliminate as many sharp curves and turns as possible for safety.

In Wyoming, the Lincoln Highway follows the general path of what is now Interstate 80, U.S. Highway 30 and State Highway 374 extending from Pine Bluffs and exiting outside of Evanston. While these modern and maintained public roads have obliterated much of the Lincoln Highway, there are still many stretches of original road that exist.

As part of my job at the time, I became very familiar with the Lincoln Highway. My first real interaction with this historic road was shortly after I started at WYDOT. In 2014, Wyoming PBS released a special called "100 Years on the Lincoln Highway". Prior to the wide release of the documentary, Wyoming PBS and the producers of the film hosted a limited evening preview to special guests at a local hotel. I attended with several other historians and local enthusiasts where we were greeted with candy bars that were in the shape of a Model T. We were treated with the sneak preview and a panel Q&A with several of the folks responsible for the production. That documentary blew me away! I was so excited to see how significant that historic road was for the country and the residents of Wyoming. That was the beginning of the end for me (or perhaps the end of the beginning).

Destin-T Takes Hold

WYDOT regularly conducted work that required I consult with the State Historic Preservation Office. There were times when I would need to work on designing an interpretive sign or brochure, salvage pieces of Lincoln High bridges, talk to resident historians about it and so forth. At some point, I think around 2018, I started researching the Ford Model T and the Model A. Both vehicles have a very rich and important history. Despite the alphabetic disharmony, the T came before the A. Based on my understanding of the controls of each vehicle, I initially wanted a Model A. The controls of a Model A are very much similar to what we think of as a modern, manual vehicle. Both the T and the A were active participants driving along the Lincoln Highway, and I started pricing them out. Lower quality Model As were comparable in price to the higher quality Model Ts, at least in my area (the prices can and do vary widely around the country for both models).

One day, while watching the local ads, a Model A came up for sale at a local car dealership. I took a coworker with me to go for a test ride. I looked over the car and it was quite clean and clearly had caring owners. The salesman let my coworker and I take it for a test drive around the block. The car started and ran well! I had serious issues grinding the gears when shifting and stalled it several times. We drove it back and I tried, unsuccessfully, to negotiate a lower price. I ended up going home carless that day. A couple of weeks later, the car was still for sale. I took my girlfriend (now wife), Emily, with me for another test drive. I had the same issues and I really was not enjoying myself. I again went home carless.

I spent many-a-weekend from then on watching Model A and Model T videos online. I was slowly drifting away from the Model A and started feeling drawn to the Model T more and more, despite what I thought were crazy and convoluted controls. History, yet again, was calling to me.

The Ford Model T was the most successful endeavor of Henry Ford. The Model T was not the first automobile of its time, but it was undeniably the most prolific for many years. Released to the world in 1908, this revolutionary vehicle fulfilled a demand people didn't know they needed. The Model T made travel accessible to the masses, something previously reserved for the wealthy. The Model T, at a paltry 20 horsepower by today's standards, replaced the horse and carriage as the primary mode of transportation (save for maybe the Amish community). The car was affordable, reliable, and extremely durable for the "roads" of the time. There were over 15 million produced during its run from 1908 to 1927. It is estimated that there are still about 200,000 Model Ts operating today.

The Model T features vanadium steel construction. The use of vanadium steel is very noteworthy as it significantly increases the hardness and tensile strength of steel. It's not widely used in modern automobiles, but it is used in surgical instruments and specialty tools where hardness is an important consideration.

The Model T has other notable features. Its ground clearance is 8 inches. The average modern all-terrain vehicle (ATV) has a ground clearance of 10 inches whereas the modern sedan has a ground clearance of around 5 inches. This allows the Model T to handle terrain of all sorts in a similar manner to that of an ATV and better than a modern passenger vehicle. The planetary transmission, which shares lubrication with the engine's oil, features two forward gears and a reverse, all of which are controlled by floor pedals. The timing and acceleration of the engine are controlled by levers to the left and right of the steering wheel. The handbrake to the left of the driver (opposite in Canadian versions of the Model T) serves as a parking brake, a clutch, a sort of neutral, and can shift into high (second) gear, depending on its position relative to the clutch pedal. Someone once said that driving a Model T is like driving a car that is always in cruise control, and I think that's a good way to think about it. My Model T has an extra shifter to the right of the driver, which shifts my Ruckstell underdrive.

A fter multiple years of watching videos online all about the history of the Model T, basic maintenance, buyer's guides, on and on and on, a rare opportunity came up that changed everything for me.

Jim and PaTience

At some point during my research, some wise advice came my way. For Model Ts, you get what you pay for and therefore you should buy the best condition car you can afford because otherwise you'll end up putting in a ton of money on a restoration project. For some people, that's exactly what they want, a project to tinker with. I, on the other hand, wanted a running and driving Model T so that I could turn around and start driving right away around town. In early March 2021, I was browsing some online advertisements when I came across a Model T for sale in Colorado, about an hour away from my house. The ad listed a 1919 Model T Touring in great condition for sale. It was running and driving with great condition upholstery and no known mechanical issues. It was in a good price range for a Model T of that year, and it was a touring vehicle! The touring style was what I was hoping for, so that I could drive around with the top down and wind in my hair (at 30 miles per hour). I closed out of the ad and moved on since I did not have any extra money and could not take out a loan at that time.

At that very time, my wife and I were in the process of getting a new home built for our fledgling family. Our son, Oliver, was just about to turn two years old and we needed more space for him than we had. My mother was also in need of care and had to live with us. Space was at a premium, so we were working on getting a new house to accommodate our specific needs. While talking about the home with our lender, I mentioned that I saw the Model T ad and had wanted to buy one but could not afford it. He suggested that we increase the mortgage slightly to cover the cost of the car. I jumped on the opportunity as fast as I could! My wife, needless to say, was not thrilled. I emailed the gentleman in the ad and eventually we spoke on the phone and set a date for me to drive down and look at the car. My wife humored me and agreed to go along with me to take a look.

In preparation for the big day, I rewatched and reread as many buyer's guides as I could. I wanted to make sure I knew exactly what I was getting myself into and that the car was a good purchase for the money. On Sunday, March 7th, 2021, we loaded up and drove south to look at the car. It was quite a drive into a rural area to Jim's house and shop. The GPS got me into the neighborhood, and I knew which property was his the moment I saw a Model T parked by the driveway as "yard art". That was a very good sign that I was dealing with someone who understood Model Ts.

Jim's shop door was wide open; after shaking his hand and making introductions, I saw not only the 1919 touring car I was interested in, but also several other Model Ts and Model As parked all over the place! I also saw a Model T fire engine! Jim told me he had been "doing Ts since 1980" and was a member of both of the clubs in the Denver area. He gave me a big tour of his vehicles and what he did to them all and talked about how he built that fire engine from a pile of parts. Jim had also restored a Model T pickup for the Snap-On Tool company, which is on display at their museum. The man checked every box you could think of for a reliable Model T owner and operator. I was very impressed and excited.

Then the focus turned toward the 1919 Touring sitting front and center in Jim's shop. "No issues with either engine or ruckstell that I am aware of." Jim says, "Drive it away". I look it over and try to keep in mind as much of the buyer's guide video tips as I could. Checking for things like rust, loose spokes, body damage, and more. The car looked very clean to me. "The body and title are 1919, but the engine is 1920, it's common to swap out engines over the years." according to Jim.

Apparently, this beauty spent many years in California. As I was told the story, it was purchased by a man in California sometime in the late 1980s. He had the engine fully rebuilt, replaced valves, rebored cylinders, aluminum pistons, and probably more. The man drove the car around for a while before realizing that he didn't much care for the Model T lifestyle. He moved to Colorado, and the car sat inside of a covered shed for over 30 years until he sold it to Jim in 2020. Jim cleaned it up and got it running. He found no rust in the gas tank, cleaned the carburetor and cleaned the upholstery. Unlike many other Model Ts, this one featured a Ruckstell. The Ruckstell is a period accessory, the only one Ford himself approved of using. The Ruckstell replaced the standard rear end differential of a Model T to provide a gear you can shift into that is in between the 1st and 2nd gears of the Model T. This allows you to better handle hills and steeper grades – typical for a lot of California driving. "Larry wanted me to pull that Ruckstell out and sell it to him" Jim stated. "You're getting a very good deal here". I did not disagree.

Jim backed out the 1919 and told me to hop in and drive it around the block with him. I figured he would drive, and I would ride shotgun. "You're buying it, you need to drive it" Jim said as he opens the only door to the front seat so I can get in. Me, not wanting to look too much like an amateur, went ahead and started to recall the many videos I watched on how to drive a Model T. I had no idea how the Ruckstell worked, so I left it alone. Jim had the car idling, so after he climbed in and shut the door, I stomped the clutch pedal to the floor to activate low gear and off we went! We drove around the neighborhood, which had a couple of straight aways where I could throw the hand level forward and drive in second gear. I remember being terrified that I was moving at an unknown speed (likely around 20 miles per hour), with the engine booming, and out on a public roadway. I managed to drive it well, with not much instruction from Jim who commented that he needed to adjust the clutch so it would shift easier into second (high) gear. After that test drive, Jim tells me he recommends I get some Rocky Mountain Brakes since I have the ruckstell, so that if it ever gets stuck in neutral, I can stop the car. Jim just happened to have a set that he wasn't using. Jim said he'd prefer I clean up the car some more while at his shop for at least a couple of weeks and that would help get any questions I had answered. When the car and I were ready (and insured), he agreed to trailer the car up north to Cheyenne for me. That worked for me, so I left my deposit and made plans to come back the following weekend.

A couple of weekends went by where I was shown how the Ruckstell worked, how the Rocky Mountain Brakes worked (hint: there's nothing extra to do once it has been adjusted), what oils to use in the engine and in the Ruckstell, and all sorts of other tidbits. I also scrubbed down the car some more, cleaned up the electrical connections to remove the built-up oxidation, replaced the broken foot starter switch, and did all I could to get it road worthy after sitting mostly undriven for 30 years. Then the big day came for Jim to trailer my new car home! She didn't have a name...yet, but "down the road" so to speak, she taught me what her name ought to be. Patience.

Jim and Patience pulled into my driveway, along with Jim's friend Larry. They unloaded Patience into my driveway and not long after, it was just me and Patience. "Now what" I thought. "What have I gotten myself into now?"

PaTience. PaTience. PaTience.

The first real hurdle, before I could go anywhere on the road with Patience, was getting her titled and registered in the great state of Wyoming. With my bundle of paperwork in hand from Jim, I made my way down to the Laramie County offices to pay the sales tax, obtain a Wyoming title, obtain plates and registration and stand in multiple lines for long periods of time. One line to pay my sales tax on the car, another line to obtain the title, this office would not give me the title until registration was paid by going through another line and then coming back to this line to show proof of payment and get the title. It was pure governmental bureaucracy at its finest. Aside from standing in line for much of the afternoon, when it came time to pay registration fees, they took the original vehicle's price into account. This was pure amusement on my part as they combed through NADA books and every vehicle pricing guide they had, only to realize that nothing went back far enough to document the original retail value of a 1919 Model T Touring. They asked me for my advice on the original retail value. I told them approximately $800, which is not all that far off, but they decided to hop onto a computer and search the internet. After about 20 minutes of searching, the office person met with their boss and then grabbed another person into a little huddle off to the side and they finally agreed to a retail value of $12,000; this price was certainly not accurate, but after standing in this one particular line for so long, then talking to them for nearly half an hour about this with still more lines to stand in, I didn't argue with them. By the close of business that day, I had a clean Wyoming title, registration, license plates and tags and Patience was ready to operate on the public roads of Wyoming.

The first few drives focused on going up and down my street, learning to shift, learning to move the levers at proper times, learning to stomp on the pedals, never letting them slip (it's bad for the transmission drums), and trying to build up confidence for the longer and more complicated drives. I also learned how much oil a Model T leaks for no good reason other than it wants to mark its territory (more than you might think). I learned to top off oil, top off coolant (it ran a bit hot), and to top off the Ruckstell (it was leaking too). In between, I had to top myself off with a beer as this work made me thirsty. Patience had some issues shifting from 'low' gear to 'high' gear and I still did not fully understand how the Ruckstell shifted. At the time, I did not know anyone other than Jim who owned a Model T. Jim was always a phone call away, but sometimes I could really use someone, in person, to help show me how it's done.

I quickly joined the forums for the Model T Ford Club of America (MTFCA) and asked a lot of questions. I also spent a lot of time scouring the internet in general. I did find some help in adjusting the clutch pedal and the handbrake for "free neutral". Once I got that dialed in, Patience could shift easily between her two main gears. It involved lots of adjustments, a new slow speed clevis connection and pin (after a century of use, the holes were wallowed out!) and lots of.... patience! In hindsight, that was one of the easier, and cheaper problems to fix. As time went on, I had to tweak, adjust, and replace more things.

One afternoon after returning from a drive through the neighborhood of our new home, I was attempting to drive up our steep driveway and park Patience in the garage. Our driveway is very steep, so I needed to get a running start with the T to avoid stalling out while not trying to drive through the house itself. I gave her some gas and all of a sudden...THUD! I got stuck on the gutter of my sidewalk. I tried to drive up and over it, into the driveway, by giving her a healthy dose of gasoline and opened up the throttle quite a bit. I heard the car's RPMs increase but I was not moving forward at all. I backed up and took another run at it with the same result. I scratched my head and got out and discovered my front passenger tire was flat. Not only had the tire gone flat, but all the aggressive ramming against the curb of my sidewalk had cracked one of the hickory spokes. I knew early on that the tires were not in good condition, 30 years of sitting in a shed someplace had caused the rubber to crack and split all over. I should have kept a better eye on my tire pressure, but in life, you learn from your mistakes, and I sure made a big one! My neighbors across the street saw me struggling and came over to help me push the car back into my garage. We fought Patience up the steep driveway and into the garage. I looked into ordering a set of new tires and researched a way to salvage the spoke on that tire. This led to a "fix" that taught me another lesson approximately one year later.

Ultimately, I was put on a waitlist for new tires. While I waited months for the four, 30 x 3 ½ tires to arrive from some factory in Vietnam, I came to the conclusion that I was not prepared to re-spoke the wheel. The other spokes were, mostly, solid on all of the other wheels and I wanted to rush back into the fray as quickly as possible. I purchased some clear two-part epoxy. I mixed some up and flowed it into the crack and pressed it together as best I could and let it cure. While not looking pretty the following day, it was rigid and seemed to solve the issue of a wiggly, cracked spoke. I should say, for the record, do not ever do that! That was a dumb move in hindsight. I came to understand how those spokes function with respect to the lateral forces a Model T endures when it makes a turn. For now, however, epoxy and a basic vulcanized tire patch got me back on the road. Thankfully, that year I was not doing any substantial drives.

New tires eventually arrived and new tubes for the inside. The replacement of a tire on the rim of a Ford Model T gives many of us a mild headache, at least at first. The tires are hard and stiff, and it takes a strong arm and a lot of finesse to do that job (anyone that says otherwise might be right but has most assuredly been doing it far longer than the average T-raveler). After letting the tires sit in the sun to warm up, I used some motorcycle tire spoons I had laying around from a past life and removed the tires. I had some minor surface rust inside the rim, so I sanded them and then repainted them silver to imitate the zinc plated appearance they would have originally had and fought for over an hour to get the new tires on. They were very stiff, and I really had no good technique to get them on. They went on eventually, and I had to make many touch ups on the paint. After dealing with the flat that broke my spoke, I made sure to fill them up to 60 PSI and I began to check all tires at the start of the driving day. I have never experienced a flat tire, from a tire that was actively driving, since (knock on wood). I need to include that caveat for something I'll get into later.

At the end of that short Model T year, I had learned how to get around quite a bit. There was a 1920s original Lincoln Highway bridge just a couple of miles down the street from my house. I took friends and family through my neighborhood, down the street, over that bridge, turned around and went back. I did that drive dozens of times that year. I shifted the Ruckstell, shifted gears, finagled all the levers, and got comfortable with short drives. There were hiccups with the car that I needed to deal with during the winter. The carburetor and timer (and timing) needed to be better adjusted. The car hesitated a lot on very small hills.

That first winter, I watched a lot of online videos and read some guides online and tore apart my Holley NH carburetor all on my own. As far as carbs go, this one is pretty basic. I drilled out some plugs in the air passages and dug out a ton of gunk. The passages were pretty well blocked from years of neglect. I repainted it and restored it. The process for that was not hard at all! It was really straightforward, and I believe any amateur could tackle that project. The timer was a poorly made New Day style timer. Lots of people love New Day timers. I have come to strongly dislike them. This was one of the infamous "S" stamped New Day timers. It is known that this particular version of the reproduced New Day Timers have a plastic casing that is too soft; it can eventually develop grooves that cause the brush (piece of copper or bronze attached to the cam shaft which completes the electrical circuit, firing each cylinder) to bounce around and cause misfires. On mine, a good groove was worn in between the internal metal contacts, which also had some carbon, and probably some melted plastic built up on the contacts. If you have a New Day, check the front of the timer. Right below the hole for the rod, check for a capital "S". If you have the "S", replace that bad boy! I bought a new, New Day timer and cleaned up that one as best as it could serve as a spare in my toolbox in the event the replacement failed.

An "S" on this New Day indicates "S"horts!

I then taught myself how to adjust the timing on the Model T. I wanted to make sure that the timing was as accurate as possible. That process was made very easy by the legendary Steve Jelf and is posted on his website, https://dauntlessgeezer.com/. After I got the timing and timer and carb cleaned and fixed, I bought new wiring harnesses and made sure all of the electrical connections were new, clean, and tight. I started Patience up in the garage and, low and behold, there were still misfires. This led me to the trembler coils.

The coils were brand new. Jim purchased a set of brand new (not refurbished) from one of the vendors when he was getting Patience ready to sell. Perhaps they needed to be tweaked, but they were brand spankin' new. Jim has an Electronic Cranked Coil Tester (ECCT), arguably the best tool available to test and tune your coils. I took them down to Jim's place and let him use his ECCT to test the coils to make sure they were adjusted. All four failed the capacitor test! Jim couldn't believe it and attributed it to some random error. Ignoring that the capacitors were testing as bad, he ran the other spark related tests and then adjusted the metal points until he was happy. They were by no means perfect according to the ECCT, but he felt that they should work. After putting them back in the car, yet again, I had misfires. People more knowledgeable than I in coils opined online that these new reproduction coils used poor quality capacitors. I ended up buying the correct "orange drop" capacitors, cut out the old ones, soldered in the new ones, and sent them off to a very fine company called Midnight Coil Repair, owned by a good man named Luke Chennell. He reported that the capacitors were fine, and he made a number of adjustments to the points, and they were all testing perfectly! I was so relieved. I got them back in the mail and immediately put them in the car and fired her up. No more misfires! The problem was gone! Patience sounded stronger than ever. I re-gapped the spark plugs and called it a day and called it a winter.

AbouT Bands and Spokes

J im had convinced me to join the Northern Colorado Model T club not long after I purchased Patience from him. Club membership has played an integral role in my ongoing education in Model Ts. In February 2021, the club had its annual planning meeting to discuss what activities the club wanted to pursue in the coming year.

Jim and I both knew that the transmission bands in my Model T were cotton, old, and fraying. It was time to replace them. Jim and I had talked prior to the meeting about me suggesting that the club put on a seminar on transmission band replacement. I mentioned that at the planning meeting, and folks seemed to like that idea. I had been toying with the idea of installing wooden transmission bands and many club members had minimal knowledge of them. Cotton and Kevlar were by far the most popular choices (Kevlar more so as cotton was not available new anymore). The plan was set! In May, the season would kick off with a seminar in transmission band replacement, featuring Patience! I was excited!

The Model T transmission system is pretty unique. Without getting into a huge technical treatise, as I mentioned, there's a reverse pedal, clutch/low speed pedal, and a brake. Each of those pedals is connected to respective bands that surround three rotating drums. Depressing a pedal causes its respective band to grip down on its respective drum inside the transmission, preventing that drum from turning. By preventing that drum from turning, it manipulates a series of gears inside the transmission and the forces of the engine are directed towards that specific pedal's objective. The bands are lined with a material that is softer than the metal of the drums so as to prevent wear. Transmission band linings started out as cotton. Over the years, improvements resulted in the creation of improved materials such as Scandinavia (tighter weave cotton), Cantex (cotton coated in a tar-like substance), cottonwood, and now Kevlar (same stuff in seatbelts). I decided to go with cottonwood for new linings because the wood was less aggressive than Kevlar, but sturdier than cotton.

I had a set of wood bands purchased well ahead of the seminar. A couple of days prior to the seminar, Jim drove up with his trailer and hauled Patience back down to his shop to have it ready to go. I drove down early on the Saturday of the seminar to help Jim and start getting set up. The turnout was great! We started the seminar by talking about the different materials and then showing a video, we found online specifically about the wooden bands and how to install them. Wood bands install differently from the other types, and you need to make sure your metal backing to the bands are perfectly round so as not to crack the wood. After the discussion, we started disconnecting the starter and the other appurtenances to facilitate the removal of the transmission cover (lovingly referred to as the "hog's head" due to its appearance). While I did the dirty work under the car, and boy was it dirty, the others stood overhead lovingly giving their support from above. We got the hog's head removed after fighting with the 15 bolts that hold it on. We moved it onto some cardboard to contain the oil dripping from it. Finally, the real work could begin. The transmission bands disconnect pretty easily once you can get into them with the hog's head off. One club member helped out by making sure the bands were round by bending them around a spare transmission drum that was laying around the shop. Several other club members gathered around the open transmission and examined the drums by slowly turning the engine with the crank. Everything looked good for the most part. The drums showed some little, tiny holes or "pitting" caused by rust at some point in their lifetime, but no one thought that the pitting was so severe as to warrant removing the entire engine to replace the drums. I worked out in the driveway of Jim's shop, cleaning up the various parts we removed with gasoline. As I have learned from working at Jim's shop on a volunteer basis over the years, gasoline makes a fantastic solvent for cleaning model T parts. With everything clean, all of the parts looked good (save for my starter). The hog's head had been repaired with a weld at some point, but it was just fine. Then we moved on to installing the wood bands.

The bands came as curled strips of cottonwood with groves down the length of each band to allow oil to travel through them. In order to mount them to the metal backings, you need to dry fit them, drill rough holes where the rivets are supposed to go, countersink the holes, install the rivets and crimp them down. Once done, we installed the bands, adjusted them so they weren't too loose or too tight, and then put the heavy cast iron hog's head back on with new gaskets. The whole shebang took two working days. It was discovered the spring on my starter was worn out and I needed to order a replacement, so we did not reassemble everything that day. It was a great time, and everyone had fun. I learned so much about bands, adjustments, the starter, and camaraderie.

By June 2022, the epoxy "fix" on my spoke was failing. The spoke was coming loose again and this time a peculiar item fell out. It was a washer that had been cut to fit where the spoke meets the rim of the wheel. Someone had shimmed the spoke at one time! It was probably a long time ago when those spokes were installed, they likely were not the correct length, so someone filled the gap with a shim. The shim had worked its way loose and the spoke was now more unsafe than before. This was a chore I wanted to try myself. After scouring the internet, I found the blueprints for what Model T folks know as a "Regan Press", a device invented by a man named John Regan that allows for a normal person to press spokes into place. I watched a video online of one of my Model T heroes, Steve Jelf, using it to press some spokes for his car. "How hard could it be?" I uttered as I watched the video. I decided to give it a try!

I bought the wood and hardware and tinkered together a Regan Press as best as I could. I am not a handyman by any stretch of the imagination. The dimensions were not quite right. I ended up 'cutting twice for every once measured', but it was close enough. I bought appropriately sized spokes from one of the Model T vendors. There are two sizes available depending on the type of wheel you have. Mine are a tad longer than the more "standard" spokes. The new spokes seemed to be a good fit and I was hopeful that this would be a somewhat straightforward process to repair my wheel. What I thought would be a weekend project, ended up taking almost two months.

I prepared the spokes by sealing them in spar urethane. I wanted to keep the natural appearance of the wood, despite the purists who demand that they be painted black. One warm Saturday, I got three coats of urethane on them and let them dry. What I neglected to consider was the tolerance of the spokes to each other. Rather than brushing it on, I straight up dipped them in the container of urethane and set them aside to dry. I forgot to consider that they are already intended to be so tight that they needed to be pressed to begin with. I got the press ready and got the spokes in a "tent" formation and started to crank down the press. It got harder and harder to crank so I got more and more aggressive with the press until one spoke cracked! I stopped to look at it and I was so upset I had to stop and come back to it. The spoke had cracked along an edge, it wasn't a big crack, but it was there. I had made sure to order an extra spoke or two just to be safe. I prepared another spoke, fit it in and pressed it again. This time, another spoke cracked. I looked really close at them this time and noticed a buildup of urethane at the ends of the spokes where they were pressing together. I realized my mistake immediately. I gave up for the weekend, the threads on the press were all worn out from the pressure and needed to be repaired anyway.

Too much urethane!

My in-laws came to visit in July, my father-in-law has some experience with wood, so he agreed to help me. He sanded down the urethane from the mating surfaces of the spokes and managed to press them into place. As he pressed down, they kept slipping out of alignment, so we used painter's tape to hold them straight in alignment before pressing, then knocked on them with a rubber mallet as they were pressed down. After several tries, they went together. We put the wheel back on the car and gave it a good spin. There was quite a bit of runout on the wheels. We played with the torque on the hub bolts and hit some spokes with the mallet and got it as best as we could, but it was not great. It worked, but not well. I had no ambition to try to replace the spokes on the other three wheels, so one wheel was natural while the others were the original painted black style. It looked a bit hokey, but I did not care at the time; my car was a driver after all and not a trailer queen. I lost a month of driving time, and I figured that the other three wheels were a problem to solve later. Little did I know that later was coming the following year.

The Clubs

As fore-mentioned, (not so subtly in the previous chapter), that the clubs have been by far the most beneficial to my enjoyment of Patience and have been a wealth of information and comradery. I have joined two clubs as a result of my Model T, the Model T Ford Club of America (MTFCA) and the Antique Automobile Club of America (AACA). Joining both clubs was not intentional on my part, but I ended up in their ranks simply be of owning my Model T. I have never regretted joining or paying my dues each year.

MTFCA

The MTFCA was established in 1965. Their Mission Statement on their website reads: The Model T Ford Club of America strives to preserve and promote the Model T Ford for future generations by educating people of all ages in the history, lore, and skills of maintenance of the car that put America on wheels" (mtfca.com). The national body has dozens and dozens of chapters under their umbrella, scattered all over the world.

Once Jim told me about the club, I immediately felt like I needed to attend a meeting and make connections. I was not fully in the loop on how common parts were, or how troublesome operating a Model T could be (it's not a big deal really), but I figured I needed to meet those people so I could learn. The nearest two chapters to me were the Northern Colorado Model T Club (Loveland, Colorado area) and the Mile-High Pedal Pushers (Denver, Colorado area). Membership was inexpensive for both chapters (and the National organization), so I joined them both.

Jim met regularly with the Northern Colorado chapter, which was the closest to me, so I figured I'd start there. They met (and still do at the time of writing) at a popular all-you-can-eat establishment in Loveland. Jim told me to come down to their next meeting and he'd introduce me around. I am an introvert by nature, so this was hard for me to do. I drove down the evening of their next meeting and found a slew of Model Ts sitting in the restaurant parking lot. "This must be the place!" I exclaimed as I parked my truck and started inside. I made my way to the meeting space in the restaurant and found a surprising amount of people! There must have been around 20 folks. I did immediately notice that I was the youngest in the room by a good 30 years, but before I could ponder that I heard Jim speak up "Jason! How's it goin?" "Hey, Jim!" I exclaimed. Jim took me around and introduced me to the room. What struck me most was the mix of women and men. I understood the men brought their wives, as the distribution of men and women was about equal, but I started to hear the women talking about Model T trips and things almost as much as the men were. The group clearly had been friends for years.

I grabbed a couple of rounds of food and between plates, different members came over and sat down with me. They talked to me about my life, my car, Wyoming, and more. When the meeting started, I got introduced as a visiting guest. The meeting included "show and tell" items, interesting stories, upcoming swap meets, tours, and their plans for the summer picnic. I felt very much welcome, and I was glad to be there.

I went to a swap meet later in the summer that was largely sponsored by the Mile-High Pedal Pushers. The event was in the parking lot of the county fairgrounds. I did not need any parts at the time, but I could not make the meetings of their chapter because they were about two hours away from me, met during the work week and I had an infant son to help care for with my wife. Loveland was just under an hour drive each way, but trying to get to the Denver area was just not easy for me to do (plus, remember my 'carsolypsy'). I figured the swap meet would allow me to meet some of those people and make introductions. The weather was very warm and sunny. There were some cars for sale, and many booths full of parts. I had no idea what the vast majority of them were, but they were the color of the automotive history (rust). I met some people that day and had a great time.

It wasn't long before I felt compelled to take my membership to the next level. I wrote to the Executive Director of the MTFCA Board of Directors in 2023 about running for membership on their board. She responded with a long list of things they'd like to make me aware of as far as commitments go. It was at that time that I had recently made a job change and I didn't feel quite ready to put myself out there as a candidate. However, the following summer, 2024, I got another email from the Executive Director asking me if I was interested in running that year. I felt ready and said yes!

It was overwhelming to see my picture and short bio in the fall issue of the Vintage Ford magazine. I was excited, though! I sent my ballot back the same day I got the magazine. I sent an email to the Northern Colorado folks, not advocating that they vote for me, but to just draw their attention to the fact that my name was on the ballot that year in the event they wanted to vote and normally do not. I also made some awareness posts on Facebook and even, unofficially in passing, at the Oak Spokes (see next section). A couple of Oak Spokes members ended up joining the MTFCA specifically to vote for me. I was honored and I hoped not to disappoint them or embarrass myself.

Late December rolled around and I got a call from the incoming MTFCA Board President that I had not landed enough votes for my own three year spot, but they had a member step down for personal reasons and I landed enough votes to fill the remainder of their term, which was one calendar year. I accepted and I was (still am) excited to have my spot among some of the most dedicated stewards of the Model T hobby.

As of this writing, early 2025, I have not done much yet, only a couple of months into this term. I am excited for what this year has to bring, and I intend to run again for my own term position later this year (not just filling in to finish someone else's term). I hope to update you, my esteemed reader, at some point "down the road".

AACA

The AACA was established in 1935. They brand themselves as "America's Car Club" and warmly welcome any vehicle into their fold that is 25 years of age or older. They are not Model T specific, but I found myself joining and I get just as much from them as I do MTFCA, just in a different way.

I had heard of a club called the 'Oak Spokes' back when I was working for the Department of Transportation and talking to various people about classic cars and the history of the area. I had never met a member of the Oak Spokes, but I did know that they were around and had a large presence in the Cheyenne Frontier Days Parade every July.

My first August with Patience, I entered her into the 2nd annual "Cars, Cigars and Guitars Under The Stars" car show. That year the car show was still outside on a large parcel of land owned by a local car dealership founder. It was a charitable car show that offered live music, classic cars, and another passion of mine, cigars! I found the combination of those things too appealing to resist. I paid my entrance fee and signed up as soon as I could earlier in the year. The summer went by uneventfully as I was still driving Patience largely around the neighborhood, but this was going to be my biggest drive yet – across town!

I knew it was getting time to sink or swim on driving Patience more extensively, so I found myself mapping out the most rural and rather circuitous route to the car show's location. I did not want to encounter other cars if I could help it as I was still very anxious about driving and I did stall every once in a while. The night beforehand I did some haphazard checks (I did not have the understanding of what to check as I do now) and I got Patience as ready as I felt I could. Me, Patience, and my Wife were ready to set out the next day.

The car show was just after midday and there was rain in the forecast. I crossed my fingers that traffic would be very light and that no rain would burden me, and after warming up Patience, my wife and I started off with her navigating on the GPS while I focused on manipulating the controls.

I made the beautiful and rural drive uneventfully. The car show attendant wanted to take my picture, but I could not quite get Patience to turn around in the amount of space I had, so they took a picture of my rear end with me waiving (a picture that was featured at the end of a commemorative calendar they made and gave to everyone who participated! Hah! Me and Patience were on a calendar!). The attendant guided me to my parking space and informed me that there was another Model T parked out there! I figured I had to take a look. After getting Patience and my wife situated in their parking space, I wandered off to find that other Model T. I found it! It was a very beautifully restored coupe and the owner, Neil, was a member of the Oak Spokes as it turned out! I looked his car over and listened to him talk about it and what he was working on with it (bands were upcoming as I recall) and he came over and looked at my car, definitely a driver and not a show car, and we chatted for a while. After some time had passed, a visitor who wandered in to look at the cars came up to mine. His name was JJ. JJ had an extensive family history in Model Ts. JJ knew right away about things that others didn't even notice, such as the random cross member under the car that was seen in 1919s and that I had a Ruckstell. "The only problem I see with your car..." JJ opined, "...is that it's not in my garage!". JJ told me more about the Oak Spokes, when they met, and that they were a chapter of the AACA. He told me to call a man named Bob, who was the president that year to get more information as he was about to depart on his honeymoon. I also met his wife Linda, and her son Buddy who came along. Such great people, all of them.

I called Bob and got the scoop that they were meeting at a local restaurant. I showed up and found my way to the group seating area of this particular establishment and found a whole room full of people! It was very much just like the Northern Colorado Model T Club! I found out that there were a couple of us who owned Model Ts, a few more that owned Model As, and even more that owned a vast variety of classics and many of these people had more than one classic car!

I was warmly greeted and introduced as a visiting guest. The similarities between this meeting and the only other car club meeting I had been to were uncanny. Discussions of car shows, the past summer picnic, and even a joint gathering of these folks and the Northern Colorado Model T club that I had missed out on by pure bad luck!

As time went on, I attended both clubs, but it was far easier for me to go to the Oak Spokes and talk regularly with them since we were in the same town. Once JJ came back from his honeymoon, we became pretty good friends. I talk to many of the Oak Spokes members on a near daily basis at times. In fact, it was not long before I ended up taking over the newsletter for the High Plains Region of the AACA which is composed of the Oak Spokes in Cheyenne, and the Hi-Wheelers in adjacent Laramie. Over the years I moved up through the officer positions in Oak Spokes and as of this writing, I am the President of the Oak Spokes and also President of the High Plains Region and still editor of the newsletter known as the "Tire Kicker".

The Oak Spokes have a massive presence in the Cheyenne Frontier Days Parade every July. Our spot in the parade line up is at times well over a block in length. That following summer after joining the Oak Spokes, I agreed to participate in the parade with the club, as most members do.

My first parade was with the Oak Spokes, and it was an experience still burned into my mind as a highlight of my Model T journey. That morning, I dressed up in my 1920's attire (members dress up in period clothes for their car). I have an unusual amount of 1920s attire; I think it's just part of my personality at times. It's also how I dressed for my wedding to Emily. Anyway, in my light-colored waistcoat and slacks, I drove Patience to downtown Cheyenne to find our spot in the parade lineup. The entire downtown area is closed to vehicular traffic on parade days because the route is so large and the pedestrians enjoying the parade number in the many thousands! As I was driving along the outskirts of downtown a car beeped its horn next to me "Hey,

Jason!! Looking good!" It turned out to be a coworker with his family on their way to find parking for the parade. I suffered from many, many car honks and waves on that drive. I found a parade official standing by a barricade who was waiving me in – almost like they knew I was trying to find my way into the parade lineup. I drove around and found my Oak Spokes compadres lining up down an entire street. I started to make my way down the line of vintage autos to get in line when someone stopped me. "We line up by the age of the car, you're up front somewhere" I was told. "Interesting" I thought. I turned around and made my way to the front and there was one other Model T up there, JJ! JJ walks over as I slow down and tells me that my 1919 is older than his 1926 Touring, so I was up front and leading the pack! I was immediately nervous, and a bit taken aback. I had never actually been in a parade before, let alone driving a car in a parade, and certainly never up front leading the entire club! I had no idea how to drive in a parade and I was betting on being able to have another car in front of me to imitate. Bob came walking up with the club's banner in the form of two giant magnet signs to stick on the side of my car. "Since you're leading, you will need these" Bob said as he affixed them to my car. We had about 30 minutes until the parade started, and about another 20 minutes until our spot in the line started to move, so I spent my time getting my 360 camera attached to my car to film the drive (a new toy I thought would make things even more fun) and talking to club members. After what felt like several seconds, but was probably closer to 45 minutes, a parade official came up to me and said "START YOUR CAR! YOU GUYS ARE NEXT!". I immediately turned behind me and shouted out "WE"RE STARTING!" down the street to the members behind me and everyone hustled to their cars and started them up. "Please Patience, don't let me down." I muttered as I tried to start her up. She fired right up (phew!) and as I got moving, I shifted into my Ruckstell's low gear. The digital speedometer I had (a bicycle computer) showed me as moving at 2 miles per hour. It was the

43

perfect speed as near idle. I was moving down the street and about to turn onto the parade route.

I made my left turn in front of the Wyoming Capitol and started down the parade route! Cheers were coming from every direction! Every couple of blocks there was an announcer who would introduce and read a prepared blurb about each organization that drove by and every time we got introduced to the crowd I laid onto my "dying duck" sounding horn and made sure Oak Spokes was loud and proud! I looked behind me to see all of the club members weaving back and forth from one side of the street to the other, honking periodically. I started doing the same. I heard people I knew shout my name from time to time. It was something I consider to be a significant moment in my life.

After about an hour, I got to the end of the parade route and the other Oak Spokes members peeled off in various directions to enjoy the rest of their day. Several members passed by me and congratulated me, which made me smile. I parked by the side of the road for a while because my car was running hot and while it wasn't overheating, I was not in a hurry, and I wanted to send some text messages to my wife and friends to let them know how it went. After a time, I started off back home, parked Patience, and spent the rest of the day feeling like a rockstar.

Cheyenne Frontier Days does four parades the week the rodeo is going on. I have done every parade, every year since. It has not desensitized me; I still feel on top of the world at each one. I am, however, a little exhausted at the end of the parade week.

I have done numerous parades now with the Oak Spokes. I have participated in mini-tours, field trips to visit museums and other member's collections, and celebrated with picnics and Christmas parties.

M embership in both clubs has been a very meaningful part of my life and has very much contributed to my success with a Model T. I very much enjoy my time with these people. JJ and his wife Linda have become good friends to me and my wife. My son looks forward to seeing Linda at each club meeting. I visit Jim regularly and go down just to help him fix up a new Model T project he bought. The access to friendly, knowledgeable people makes it possible to enjoy these cars without feeling overwhelmed. A Model T can be a finicky car and having access to people who have been there before keeps the frustrations to a minimum. If you are not a member of any clubs, you need to correct that error right away!

T-Curse of Pine Bluffs - 2022

I have enjoyed myself every time I have been in Pine Bluffs. I hold no ill will towards the town. However, every trek I have thus far made to Pine Bluffs in Patience has resulted in character building for myself, and character rebuilding for Patience. There is just something about the town that challenges the patience of myself and...Patience.

Pine Bluffs, Wyoming rests along Interstate 80 right at the border of Wyoming and Nebraska. Pine Bluffs is small, with a population of 1,121 in 2023. There are few amenities in the town, but quite a few attractions. Arguably the biggest draw is distillery, which hosts frequent events and has a tasty selection of locally distilled whiskey. The town is small, but mighty! Annually, the first weekend in August, the town hosts Trail Days. It is your typical small-town celebration with a parade down the main drag, music, and vendors and fun! It's a huge draw in August and in election years, you better believe every politician in the surrounding area who is serious about running for office has a float and makes an appearance.

I had never been to Trail Days prior to owning Patience. It's a 37-minute drive at 80 miles per hour down I-80 from my house, not far, but I just never made the trip. Not long after I got to driving Patience around on a more regular basis, I started looking for fun drives and things to do. I thought about Trail Days and pulled up a map. The I-80 access road runs parallel to the interstate for the length of the trip from my house to Pine Bluffs, and is a well-paved road that I could drive at 35 miles per hour with only a couple of small turns along the way, but passing by multiple gas stations along the way. All in all, it is a perfect trip for a Model T in almost every way you could ask.

Starting in Winter 2021/Spring 2022, I started planning for the trip and I was excited to stretch my legs and also get some exercise for Patience. March that year had several very warm days for southeastern Wyoming. One day my friend John and I got to talking about how we enjoyed whiskey and scotch, but John had not indulged in it for some time, and I am always on the lookout for a good whiskey. I don't believe he had been to Pine Bluffs Distillery at the time, and I certainly had not so we talked about going over some weekend to give them a try and see what they had to offer. With the weather being so nice and itching to get Patience out of the garage to awaken her from her winter slumber, I suggested driving over in the Model T. John thought that sounded like a fun time, so we planned for an upcoming Saturday that was intended to be sunny and warm. We planned for a late-morning departure to get over to Pine Bluffs, find some food, sample some whiskey at the distillery, then head back before the sun set and it got cold. The nights were still very cold in March and an open car did not sound very fun in such conditions.

The morning was ideal! The sun came out early and warmed Cheyenne almost right away. I got Patience out into the driveway and did the standard pre-drive checks: oil, coolant, and tire pressure. I started the car and got her warmed up. All systems were go! John came over, parked his modern car at my house and we hopped into Patience and off we went...to the gas station! We stopped at the gas station right on the access road that leads out of town to top off the tank. Finally! We were on the open road! I didn't have the car all dialed in at that time just yet. On that drive, Patience would not move faster than 32-35 miles per hour no matter what, throttle wide open. That did not matter. The top was down, and the access road had moments of good scenery along the way. Occasionally, a semi-truck passing along the adjacent interstate would lay on its horn in honor of us. Passing cars on the access road would wave and smile at us. Patience was an instant smile-mobile. John and I were smiling, enjoying the warm wind and fresh air. We stopped at another gas station, at approximately the halfway point. I pulled into the station and started gassing up. "that car is amazing!" came a shout from the pump adjacent to us "thank you!" I said. They were two teenagers driving a truck next to us. John was chatting up one of the two while I was talking to the other. I showed him the engine, and hand crank and he loved it. He took some pictures on his cell phone. I buttoned up the gas tank, put the seat back on (gas tank is under the front seat which amuses a lot of people) and John and I said our goodbyes and we set off again. We ended up using the GPS on our phones to find the appropriate turns along the way. There were a lot of local county roads that branch off of the access road and we did not want to get lost. After about an hour and a half we pulled into Pine Bluffs! It was probably just after lunchtime, and we decided to skip lunch for the distillery and have an early dinner instead. We drove along an amazing dirt road out to the distillery which is something straight out of a movie. It was (and is) beautiful county, especially to be parking a Model T in. I decided not to park in one of their designated spots and instead parked out at the edge of their property, near the road in. I did not want the car to somehow roll away into something or not start and need to be pushed out of the way or any number of other concerns I had about parking right next to some other modern cars. I chocked the wheels to be safe and inside we went!

Pine Bluffs Distillery is amazing. We sat down at the bar and we each ordered a flight of various samplings. The very friendly staff gave us an overview of the differences between wheat and rye and how the different whiskeys are made in house using locally-sourced ingredients. We sampled a lot of their wares. We spent some time chit-chatting here and there with various folks coming in and out, some of them commenting on the Model T parked out front. We slowed down after a bit and spent a couple of hours drinking some water and passing time until we felt ready to get dinner.

Plans for an early dinner turned into plans for a normal-hour dinner as we paid our tab and prepared to drive back into the center of town to find something to eat. As I went outside to get Patience up and running, I was greeted by a small crowd of several people that had gathered around Patience and were looking her over from top to bottom. "That is such a cool car!", and "What year is it" were immediate questions that I addressed. They had never seen it in the area before, so they asked where I drove in from. "We came over from Cheyenne for the day" I declared. "You drove that car THAT far? WOW!" John and I got invited to come back for the "Corgi Derby" that the distillery hosts at the same time as the Kentucky Derby as a fundraiser for the animal shelter. "Your car would fit in perfectly and many people dress up fancy for the event" I was told. John and I said that there was a chance we could come back and hoped to see them all again soon.

As it turns out, restaurant options were few and far between in Pine Bluffs and options get slim real fast as the day goes on. Most places we could find were already closed for the day or had oddball hours. We spent some time on our phones and found a locally owned Mexican restaurant that was open, and we stopped in to get some dinner. We had some good dinner and at some point, near the end of dinner, John accidentally bumped his full water cup over. Cold ice water made its way rapidly across the table and then down onto my pants. I quickly became soaked. We scrambled to clean it up with napkins and contain the water, but my pants had already succumbed to the cold moisture. I didn't worry too much about it, and we paid our bill and left. We topped off the gas at the station next to the restaurant and by then the sun was gone. It was chilly. We had a long drive ahead in an open car, at night. I asked John to look up directions to get us back to the access road to get home. It was dark and I was all turned around. John's phone was having a hard time getting a signal so we did the best we could.

We ended up doing several loops around town trying to find the way out. We started down one road for about half an hour before realizing that none of the surrounding area looked familiar. We stopped, turned around and drove half an hour back to town to start over again. I was getting irritated at myself for not knowing the way. Patience was teaching me her most believed virtue and teaching it well. The whole time my legs were getting colder and colder as the temperature was dropping outside. I pulled over and dug out my phone and started to look for directions. I found the path and got us on the road.

After about an hour of failed attempts to get on the road home, we were finally, actually, on the real road home! We did not get the top up on the car and I just wanted to get home so I opened the throttle as much as I could and quickly encountered two issues. The winds that had hit me at 35 mph were quite literally freezing my legs. My jeans had not dried at all after the ice water bath and these breezes were cold! The ambient temperatures were somewhere in the 40s meaning the winds were biting at temperatures not far off from freezing. I was shivering and shivering and shivering. The second issue was my headlights. I knew they needed some work, one headlight had a short in it and they both were not very bright but this problem was more pronounced in an area where collisions with wildlife was a real possibility and there was no way I could stop as fast or as reliably as a modern vehicle.

Above: this is what I was working with for headlights on my very first unintended nighttime drive in the country.

———◆———

I was essentially fueled by two motivations that night. The first was the desire to not lose my legs to frostbite (a bit of an exaggeration, but it was cold and my legs were getting numb!) and the second was the adrenaline of having my head on a swivel trying to keep an eye out for wildlife to avoid a collision. We stopped at the same gas station at the midpoint again. I topped off the tank and we loitered inside for a few minutes to warm up. It was about 40-45 minutes back to my house from this point at 35 mph. It was taking a little longer because I was driving a bit slower at times out of caution not being able to see down the road in any meaningful way with what was equivalent to a single D-cell flashlight for a headlight. Finally, after an evening backcountry drive that I felt every second of, we were on the outskirts of Cheyenne!

As we were entering town, a semi-truck gave us a final surprise. I was accustomed to cars getting close to my rear end for a few moments, then pulling over into the next lane to pass. Often that driver and I would wave at each other, and it was understood by your average driver that old cars cannot go fast. This time it was a semi-truck. It pulled up on my butt so fast at first, I thought it was going to hit us. Right as it was about to, it quickly braked, fell back about three car lengths, and matched my speed. I was trying to keep an eye on it in my mirror and it just followed at that speed and never tried to pull over. It followed us as we made a turn and started towards my neighborhood! At this point, I had concerns that perhaps this guy had road rage and was going to confront us. I pulled into the subdivision where my house was, and the semi-truck continued to follow us! It was not a delivery van, but a huge, freight hauling, semi-truck that clearly did not belong in a residential subdivision. I yelled over to John that I was not going to let this guy follow us to my house and I was going to keep driving through the subdivision until we lost him, or he moved on. John had noticed the same thing as I did and suggested, partly in jest, that if he got on top of us, we should stop the car, bail out, and run in different directions! Neither of us felt like potentially having a fight with a truck driver caffeinated out of his mind or worse. I did a couple of quick loops down some streets in the subdivision, and we lost the semi-truck. We got around the corner to start back towards the correct streets to my house and saw the semi-truck backing up, then heading back towards the entrance to the subdivision. We had no idea what was going on with the guy, but we were glad to see him leaving. I pulled Patience into my garage and shut her off. We both sat there. I don't know what John was thinking, but I had conflicting thoughts of excitement over the first half of the day combined with the not-so-fun drive home and strange encounter with the semi-truck. John and I chit-chatted about the events of the day for a few minutes then he called it a night and went home. I needed to warm up, so I went inside and did the same thing. I had survived my first substantial drive, Pine Bluffs had nearly frozen me, but did not break me – yet.

The rest of the summer driving season went by without issue; but the upcoming Trail Days tour was something I had been looking forward to. I did love that drive; I was also excited to go back and drive in the parade and attend a car show that was scheduled to take place at the local bar right afterwards. The Oak Spokes Antique Car Club had a spot in the parade and one other fellow member was interested in going with me. He wanted to drive his Model A, which can do speeds much faster than my Model T. I didn't want to hold him up, so I told him I would just meet him there at the parade and we could represent the club and attend the car show. The plans were made!

My wife has a friend who lives not far outside of Pine Bluffs, and she wanted to be in the parade with me along with our son. She mentioned I could drive to her house the night before and park my car there so that I would not have as far to go on the morning of the parade. I thought that sounded fine, so I drove over to her house the night before and my wife followed me in her modern car to take me home. That drive went very smoothly. I got Patience parked and tucked in for the night.

The following morning, we got up and everything was chaotic. We rushed around to get candy for the parade, chairs, water, sunblock, everything you could imagine for a day outside in the sunshine for 3 very fair-skinned people. We left home and drove to Patience. She had slept well. She had a little moisture on her from some the cool night previous, so I wiped her down and got her started and warmed up for the last little jaunt into Pine Bluffs. I queued up the GPS on my phone and started off. It took about 20 minutes, and I had to drive around town a bit to find my way around the parade route to the staging area. I pulled up and found my friend from the Oak Spokes parked in our spot. As is the tradition in Oak Spokes, the cars line up for parades, oldest first, so I pulled ahead and prepared to lead the way for our group of two.

Above: Patience is ready to go!

We had some vintage cars ahead of us and behind us, but they were with other clubs along with some politicians who came out to stump ahead of their November elections. I chit-chatted a bit and went over Patience's tires and checked for leaks and just overall nervously poking at her ahead of the start. The parade route is short as far as parades go. The route goes about half a mile for the length of Main Street. It's not a long parade, but it is fun! The signal was given and everyone fired up their cars, trucks, go-karts, tractors, everything and started moving at about 2 miles per hour. Patience started up well. I threw her into "Ruckstell High and Ford Low" which lets me drive at just about the perfect speed. The Ruckstell makes parades so much easier. As I drove my wife and her friends up the parade route, they were throwing candy, and the kids were nothing but smiles. My son, Oliver, was having a great time tossing (and eating) candy along the way. The girls got a little excited and had tossed out all of their candy by about the halfway point, but fortunately there were plenty of other drivers who had candy to toss out. The whole thing was over for us after about 25 minutes.

Short but sweet! I drove down the street and doubled back to where we started to drop off my wife, son, and friends so they could go on about their day in a modern car. My Oak Spokes partner, John (not the same John from the first trip), already knew to meet me over at the "Knotty Pine Saloon" for the car show, so I just proceeded to drive up the street to the saloon to enjoy a beer and car show!

I was one of the first ones to pull up to the car show, I believe John was first. One of the car show attendants guided me into a parking spot and I hopped out to go register. Admission was free! After finding John, we walked around and looked at the cars pulling in and getting set up.

It was about 10:30 and the car show winners would not be announced until 2. The distillery was not a good walking distance away from the saloon, so we had a couple of beers and stayed at the saloon. Some of the politicians came for a little while and were fun to talk to. No matter what you may think of them, they all seem to have silver tongues. It was a nice way to pass some time. I also really got to know about John, his rich life history and the years he spent working in the medical profession both locally and internationally. The man is beyond smart and at the age where he doesn't mince words when it comes to various policies on things both State and nationally. The man is interesting! Eventually, it was time for the winners to be announced! I won nothing, but John won Best in Show for his restored Model A. I was happy for him! He has a nice car. After the show was over, I made a real quick stop at the distillery to pick up one of their limited-edition releases that they do special for Trail Days, and then John and I started back home along the access road.

I was in the lead going home. It is good practice to put the slowest cars at the front, so they don't get left behind by the faster cars. John kept a nice distance behind me, about three car lengths or so. I was driving full throttle with a very warm breeze blowing by me and sunshine above. It was about as ideal a drive as you could hope for. I was getting a little dehydrated from the events of the day, drinking from a water bottle next to me and nothing remarkable was happening. All of a sudden, my car started to slow down. As I moved the throttle around, my speed was not changing. I then noticed that my engine had stopped puttering! I pulled over to the side of the road and hopped out to look under the hood. Right as I got the hood opened up, John had parked and got out. "You were leaking quite a bit of what looked like coolant" he declared. I looked under the car and saw a lot of coolant spewing out of the overflow on the radiator. Given the Model T coolant system is not pressurized, I had no concerns opening up the radiator cap to look inside. I used a handkerchief to turn the cap loose as it was scalding hot. Once I got it off, steam was spewing out of the radiator. Using the flashlight on my phone, I looked inside and saw no fluid at all. Somehow, I had overheated and lost, or boiled off, all of my coolant. I sat there for a time to let everything cool. John had sat with me. Fortunately, we had passed a gas station not more than 10 miles back,

I knew I could get more coolant once the car calmed down and get myself home. While waiting, a couple of nice people stopped to ask if we needed help. We thanked them for stopping but told them we were just waiting for my engine to cool down some.

After a little while, I looked around to see what water I had to refill the radiator. I did not have any coolant, nor did I have any distilled water with me. I had some drinking water from earlier. I dumped in about a gallon of drinking water I had, and John agreed to follow me back about 10 miles to the gas station to get some coolant. I took it slow and steady. It was good timing because as I was coming up to the gas station, I was losing engine power again. I pulled in and went inside the gas station. No coolant. No distilled water. They had some gallon jugs of drinking water, which is ordinarily a no-no for a radiator, but I considered this to be an emergency, and I just needed to get Patience home. I bought several gallon jugs of water. It took almost four to fill up the radiator. I saw no leaks, so I figured some gunk was just blocking up some of the tubes in the core, hopefully an easy fix later on, as long as I had no engine damage from the overheating.

John and I topped off the gas tanks while we were there and then started off home. About 40 – 45 minutes later, I was pulling into my driveway. Water was coming out of the overflow tube, and I could hear the boiling inside the radiator when I pulled into the garage. As the sun was going down, I crossed my fingers, hoping that nothing was critically wrong with Patience, and went inside to call it a day.

The following day, I knew I had some work to do. I disconnected the radiator and completely removed it. I set that problem aside to deal with later. My goal was to get the head of the engine off to see what she looked like. Sooty! I saw lots of carbon buildup on the pistons, but no damage. I cleaned up the carbon and took a sign of relief as I saw no damage. I felt no scarring on the cylinder walls. I felt really lucky. I think the engine had stopped itself before it could cook itself to death.

Above: Cleaned up and feeling grateful

After getting the head back on, I turned to the radiator. I flushed it out with a garden hose and some rusty crud did come out, but I had a hard time believing that the handful of chunks was the cause of random substantial overheating. The following day, I called around to find a radiator shop that would help me. I found a shop nearby in Laramie, Wyoming that agreed to look at it, but made no promises. I drove it over and met with the guy running the shop. He told me the radiator was way too old for him to work on, but he would dip it to clean out the gunk, spray paint it and give it back with no warranty on the work. I agreed, I didn't expect him to take it apart to re-core it anyway. I was hoping he would "rod it out", by running some rods through each tube to make sure the scale was gone, but I would take what I could get. He said it would take him a couple of days to get to and he'd call me. The following weekend, I went to pick it up. It looked pretty good and I got it home, installed it, and drove it up and down the street to see if it was overheating. I carried an instant-read thermometer with me to take readings at the inlet and outlet to see if it was boiling. Having the thermometer was not really necessary, as I could see and hear the boiling again. I parked Patience and let her cool off for the rest of the day. I was frustrated and needed a break anyway. The following morning, I saw a puddle of coolant under the car. After refilling the radiator again, and looking close with a flashlight, I could see droplets forming at several places within the core. Apparently, the years of dirt and grime were actually holding the radiator together! Without the gunk, little holes were exposed at various points within the core where the metal had worn thin over the years. The radiator was toast! It needed to be re-cored or replaced and both options were expensive. I was really feeling low about the situation.

After doing some research, a re-core of the radiator was just shy of the cost of a new one. Further, I could not locate a shop that would re-core a Model T radiator within a reasonable drive from me. Sadly, this was not long after one of the popular Model T radiator companies had closed up shop, leaving me with just one vendor left who still made brand new radiators. I placed an order with Brassworks, who informed me that there was a six-month lead time on my radiator. As it was getting into fall and winter was coming, I did not have an issue with that. I would wait patiently, with Patience, for her new radiator to come in the spring.

The winter was not unproductive. I had decided to make it my mission to never overheat again! I got a new, sealed bearing fan pulley, new radiator hoses, and a new petcock for the bottom of the new radiator. Finally, in May, six months to the week from when I ordered the radiator, it arrived! I had never seen such a beautiful sight! I looked it over from head to toe – flawless. I immediately installed it and gave it a test warm-up in the garage for about an hour. No noticeable issues! I took her on a drive through the neighborhood and pulled her over with my instant-read thermometer and the hoses were well under boiling. I felt so relieved to have that problem behind me. I knew I was ready to try Pine Bluffs again the following August.

Above: Out with the old (right), in with the new (left)

No more overheating!

T-Curse of Pine Bluffs - 2023

During the winter months while Patience slumbered without her radiator, I had periodically gone down to see Jim and attend some Model T club meetings. Jim would whisper to me that a club needs activities in order to thrive, not just eat dinner once a month; a club needed to get out and do something periodically. As the new year entered, we were approaching another of the club's annual planning meetings. Jim had told me in passing that years and years ago they had done an overnight trip to Cheyenne and then over to Pine Bluffs for the parade. He didn't need to beat around the bush much more than that. Jim had given me my marching orders for the coming year. I knew the radiator was en route by Spring and Trail Days wasn't until August, so I thought "oh hell, why not?" I told Jim I would organize a tour for the club to come up to Cheyenne and then make a trip over to Pine Bluffs for Trail Days that August. I was not able to attend the planning meeting due to weather, but Jim sent me a text the evening of that meeting to tell me the club agreed to let me plan a tour for them for Trail Days. I was nervous and excited. I knew I did not have a ton of planning to do, but there were some logistics to manage: the route, a hotel for the night, the parade and car show afterwards. There were people I needed to call, and arrangements to be made. It being February at the time, I did not feel rushed, and I felt like I could get something really fun planned out in the ensuing months. So, I got to it!

At the club meetings that followed my agreeing to take on this task, members were offering me very good tips and advice. I struggled with a good route and whether or not to overnight in Cheyenne or overnight in Pine Bluffs. Most of the club was coming up from the Berthoud, Colorado general area, a handful were driving their Model

Ts the whole way and a handful of the members were trailering their cars up to Cheyenne.

Ultimately, I resolved to have them come up for lunch the Friday before Trail Days, eat, offer a couple hours for hotel check-ins, then have everyone go over to the historic Cheyenne Depot Plaza for the weekly "Fridays on the Plaza" event the city held each week during the summer. That offered food trucks, beer, live music, and some very good people watching in sunny warm weather. I figured we could get up early and trek over to Pine Bluffs on Saturday morning, do the parade, do the car show, hit the distillery, and trek back to Cheyenne where everyone could then go home. I had an itinerary with everything mapped out both the route and the amount of time for each activity. It fell into place pretty smoothly and the club membership seemed to be looking forward to it and so was I. Fun times were to be had by all! At least it started out that way...

The summer had gone by swimmingly! I had participated in several parades and car shows that summer all without any overheating or any other weird mechanical issues. I even won my first trophy at a car show! I got 2nd place in the "Classics" category of the local trampoline park's fundraising car show. The only issues I had that year were with timers. I burned through two New Day timers in rapid succession. The reproductions are trash, in my honest opinion. After installing a new Anderson-style timer, I had no further issues or misfires. Patience and I had a great summer and were looking forward to the capstone event for us, which was Trail Days. I made sure to take time off of work so I could get the car cleaned and ready and then go meet the club members in downtown Cheyenne for an afternoon of fun before the big driving day.

I got downtown and saw Model Ts dotting the street parking spaces all over! I was so excited; I was grinning from ear to ear watching pedestrians stop to look at the various club members' cars scattered all around the downtown area. I ended up parking a couple of streets away and walked into the restaurant for lunch. Some of the club members were already getting beers and others were waiting for our table. After a warm welcome, we waited around for a while and then got seated and enjoyed a great lunch filled with very good comradery.

Once lunch was over, we took a break for everyone to check into their hotel with plans to meet up at the Cheyenne Depot Plaza for "Fridays on the Plaza". I drove my Model T home and returned a couple of hours later. Much of the group was already gathered and were talking. We spent the late afternoon and early evening listening to live music, eating food, and just enjoying the nice time together. I had no inkling about the events of the following day.

About seven the following morning, I drove Patience across town to the hotel where the group was staying. Everyone was in the parking lot getting their cars ready. A couple of the members were unloading from their trailer, while others were warming up their cars and doing their pre-trip checks. It's always important to check your oil and tires before a big drive with these cars and carry spares of nearly everything with you. As I have mentioned, disaster can strike when you least expect it. I think Murphy's law comes into play on these things too. Jim was struggling to get one of his cars started. I walked over to him to see what was going on. He asked if I had a wooden screwdriver so he could short out each spark plug to see if one was misfiring. As a matter of fact, I had a wooden screwdriver in my tool bag! I ran back to my car and grabbed it and returned. Jim proceeded to short each spark plug to the head of his engine and said he thought that he had a bad trembler coil (buzz coil). As it turned out, I also had a spare trembler coil too! I sprinted back and returned again. I left it with him and walked around to check on everyone else.

Everyone else was just about in a line, in the parking lot and ready to go. I walked back over to Jim who gave me back my screwdriver and coil and said he had given up and could not get the car roadworthy and would have to drive the spare car he brought with him. Yes, you read that right, the man brought a spare car with him. He had intended for another club member to drive it, but decided they would just ride together. It was time to go and no more time to waste!

As this was my tour, I was at the front of this impressive old-timey convoy. I led us out of the hotel parking lot and through the outskirts of Cheyenne over to the interstate access road. The weather was perfect! A near cloudless day with warm sunshine and very little wind – rare in this part of Wyoming. Once I got us to the other side of town, right on the outskirts, I stopped at the gas station for everyone to catch up. That was my plan, to stop at each gas station along the way to let folks catch up, they were all well-spaced apart from each other. Once we all gathered again, I realized that I needed to slow down a bit. I had really opened up my throttle as we were running a little behind, but not everyone's car could move as quickly as mine. I resumed the journey and kept pace right at 30 miles per hour. We were coasting and cruising our way to Pine Bluffs! I felt like I was on top of the world! I had a line of nearly a dozen Model Ts behind me, on our way to the parade, and the weather was perfect. Perhaps it was the pride, but I intend to blame the curse of Pine Bluffs for the rest of my day...

"HUH?", "No way!", and several swear words came out of my mouth as I focused on what I was seeing. I gazed upon my driver's side rear wheel, or rather, where a wheel used to be when I started driving that morning. The line of cars all slowed and stopped as I had literally jumped out of my car and started looking at the jagged piece of axle that used to have a wheel bolted onto it. "What happened?" someone said. "Broken axle." Said another. "I saw your tire fly away over there!". Another club member came walking up with my wheel. "Looks like a chunk of the axle is still attached. It must have snapped from fatigue". Along with the busted axle, I had more loose spokes as a result of those spacers someone inserted years ago popping out, my backing plate for the Rocky Mountain Brakes had been folded in half and my Rocky Mountain brakes were bent. That's all the damage that I could visually see. I told the others we were less than a mile from town, they should go on as the parade started in a few minutes. They all decided to stay. It made me feel both good and sad at the same time. I knew the day was over for me, and the parade was going to be over for them. Thankfully, I had cell reception. I called my wife who was on her way to potentially drive me home. I then called Hagerty, who I was insured with, to send help. Hagerty did an absolutely fantastic job all along the way for me in this experience. I am forever grateful to them. On a Saturday morning, they found a tow truck in nearby Sydney Nebraska, to come get me. It took them about an hour to call around on their end to get me help. While I waited, the other club members were talking, eating their parade candy, checking out their own cars, and of course, coming over to look at mine and offer condolences for joining the Broken Axle Club. "It happens" I was told, along with "You are lucky you did not flip over!". I did realize that I actually was rather lucky that with the jostling of the railroad crossing at 30 miles per hour, and the sudden fracturing of my axle, I did not roll the car. Another club member noticed a bolt loose on his muffler and was fixing that issue while I waited for the tow truck to come. I smirked with jealously at his situation compared to mine.

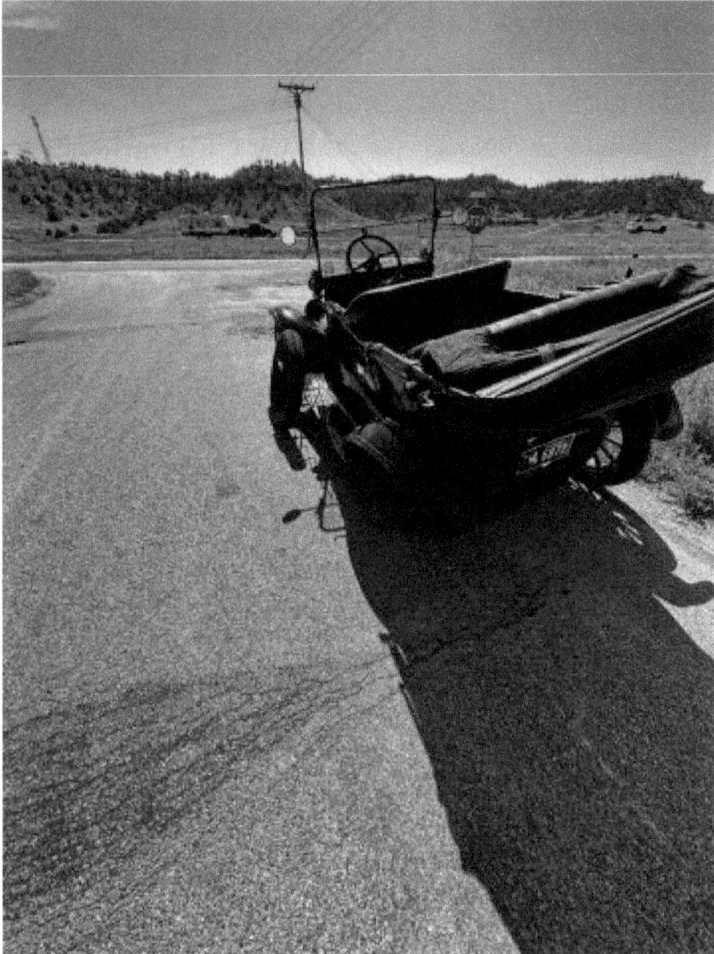

After an hour, my wife arrived. The tow truck was also en route to me. The other club members felt comfortable that I was going to be okay and they went on into Pine Bluffs to enjoy the rest of their day and the festivities. The tow truck arrived after about two hours and provided the highlights of my afternoon. "BOY, you sure got yourself in a pickle! You are missing a wheel! I am not sure how to even get this thing loaded onto my truck!" He rooted around in the back of his truck for a while looking for something. He guilt tripped me in his own way over how much easier it would have been to tow this up onto his flatbed if I had all four wheels by which to move the car. He finally found some spare pieces of flat steel that he placed under the broken part of the axle that was resting on the well-worn asphalt. I made sure the car was in high gear, gas shut off, and battery disconnected for travel. He then slowly, SLOWLY, hoisted Patience up into the bed, stopping to adjust his scrap steel here and there. After another 45 minutes. Patience was loaded onto his flatbed. My wife went on home to make sure the garage was open and ready to hopefully ease the Model T back into it. I hopped into the cab of the tow truck driver's truck, at his request. I was more than willing to head home with my wife, but he said he wanted me along for the ride. Boy was it a ride.

It was about 40 minutes back to the house from where I was. In that time, I had one of the most interesting conversations I had experienced in a long time. The man did not have a GPS, nor a "smart" phone, so my presence was needed since he had no idea where I lived and was from Nebraska. That made sense. Then I learned about his near-death experience. Apparently, while hauling a load one day a couple years prior, a semi-truck had made some sort of abrupt stop in front of him while on the interstate. He rear ended the semi, causing his load to come up from behind while his cab crumpled up in front of him. His chest caved in, with broken ribs, he died. He talked about angels, white lights, and all that good stuff you hear about with someone who had a near-death experience. He was successfully resuscitated and woke up in the hospital. It took him more than a year to recover, but he did, and he was no longer afraid of death. We also talked about his career and various other things, but once you talk about meeting angels, everything else is just boring.

We got to my house, and he excitedly backed up into my driveway to dump Patience right into my garage. I have a two-car garage and my wife's car was already parked in her spot, leaving the tow truck driver one car's worth of space to work with. After another half hour or more of tweaking his parking angle, and slowly, SLOWLY, lowering and lining up the car so it would come straight off without hitting my wife's car, he declared he was going to essentially drive forward and let it slide off. He lowered the rear of the car onto the ground, slackened up his tow chains, and with his ramp down, drove forward SLOWLY. With a bang, crash, thud, Patience slumped off onto the garage floor, axle slipping off the scrap steel in the process and gouging a deep scar into the concrete garage floor. After saying goodbye to my angelic savior, I was left alone in the quiet, standing next to poor Patience whose broken axle was now leaking oil onto the floor. The sun was getting to be low in the sky and I was so overwhelmed and overstimulated from the day, I decided to go inside and figure out next steps the next day. That evening, I spoke to Jim who told me everyone had fun in Pine Bluffs, made it home safely, and not to sweat the axle as he had plenty of parts and thanks for the great tour!

The following day, I spoke to Jim on the phone again. He told me to get the axle off and bring it to him and we would fix it. I thanked him and said I would do that. I needed to speak to Hagerty first, get more pictures, and then I could get it off and over to him. That Monday, I filed a claim with Hagerty for a "collision with a fixed object". They sent a local company to come and assess the damage for their estimate on what they would pay. After about another week, the claims adjuster came, took photos, we talked about what happened and what parts were noticeably damaged and he said they would let me know how much they would pay once they got back to the office and were able to do some research. Fine with me. I read some Ford materials and realized how easy it actually was to remove the axle along with the driveshaft. I got everything disconnected and removed in a couple of hours. I got everything over to Jim's shop where we took everything apart further to look for anything that needed to be replaced. The insurance money covered all of the new parts I needed to buy and I was able to use two axle ends that I got from Jim and JJ for free.

Aside from the broken parts from the accident, we found babbitt thrust washers inside which were in great condition but still were a must replace item. Babbitt is a tin/copper/antimony blend that Ford used mainly as a wearing surface in the engine where we would use hard bearings today. The Model T rear end also had large babbitt washers that over time flake apart and can really damage gears. I purchased new bronze thrust washers as replacements. Everything else was in largely good condition and did not need to be replaced.

After going over to Jim's shop for a couple hours every Saturday for about a month, the axle was repaired and ready to be taken home and reinstalled. I hauled it home with the axle separated from the driveshaft so that it would fit easier into my truck. When I got it home, I slapped some gasket sealer on the cardboard gaskets and bolted it all together to reinstall the next weekend.

That week at work, I had dislocated my knee in a 50-foot fall. My leg was swollen, but not broken, with a lot of fluid buildup in my knee. I did not want to put off the axle reinstall any longer than needed because it was already the end of the first week of October and the weather was quickly getting sketchy in Cheyenne. Doing this task in a standard sized garage with rain or snow going on would make the task exponentially more terrible. I called up my friend John who was more than willing to come over and help me out. The next Saturday after I finished my MRI, I flopped around on the garage floor under the Model T like a fish out of water trying to line up the universal joint inside the drive shaft with the transmission, while John slowly guided the whole thing forward trying not to cut my fingers off. We traded places after I struggled for a while then and pressed myself against the "pumpkin" of my differential while John tried to guide it in. Success! Four bolts to the transmission and the driveshaft was reattached! After some painkillers and sleep, I got the rest of it all buttoned up on my own. I could not drive Patience with my leg the way it was, so I put her on some jack stands and started her up. The wheels were turning! By the end of October, she seemed to be good to go drive again, despite the many loose spokes on the three wheels I did not repair the year prior. That was a serious issue that needed to be dealt with during the winter.

The rear axle has a planetary gear system, just like the transmission.

Reassembly begins

A month later, the swelling was under control, and I was able to drive the Model T while still struggling to get in and out. I took Patience on a test drive by participating in Cheyenne's annual Holiday Parade, which is always the Saturday after Thanksgiving. The parade was bitter cold! I had to drive across town to the parade route downtown and then drive home afterwards. We had to stage two hours early for the parade so staff could make sure everyone was lined up where they should be and that everyone had passed their safety check (mainly that you had a fire extinguisher, not that you'd have needed one as it had snowed the previous day and the temps were below freezing). I waited with the other poor souls who came with me (fellow Oak Spokes members) in the adjacent public library until they closed and kicked us out. It was so cold in my touring car, I swore off doing any more parades that late into the year, but Patience drove perfectly fine! She did not overheat (haha), and there was no issue with the differential grinding or doing anything other than puttering along. After the parade, I parked Patience and put her back on jack stands, not only for the winter at this point, but to resolve the pesky issue of many loose spokes that needed to be replaced.

Replacing the spokes was an adventure I was willing to pay someone to do at this point. I had a little cash left over from the insurance payout to accomplish the spoke replacements, which were the last of the damage from the car accident three months prior. I just needed to figure out who could do it and what I needed to do to get it to happen.

After much research and phone calls, I settled on an Amish man in Baltic, Ohio. Noah Stutzman. He has a fantastic reputation for fixing anything wood. After a couple of back and forths over the phone, I had the information from him I needed. Now, I just needed to knock out the old broken spokes, have the rims sandblasted and then painted, ship the rims to Noah, and let him handle the rest. After a weekend with a hammer, all of the spokes fell out. I say fell out because after I knocked the first loose one out, the others came tumbling along too. It was clearly another tragic accident waiting to happen, so I was thrilled to get this work done. I got the rims prepared, I got everything boxed up and in the mail! Noah called me to confirm that I wanted him to supply the bolts and also to let me know he discovered that one of the rims was out of round! I agreed to the extra work (because why not), and he said I'd have them no later than the week next. Sure enough, the wheels came just under two weeks later. With shipping time, the whole thing took about a month and with winter in full swing, it was perfect. I was floored by the legendary quality of Amish work. Everything was so tight that I had no doubt in the safety of my repaired wheels. I decided to put three coats of boiled linseed oil on them and then five coats of spar urethane to protect them. I wanted them naturally colored and not painted black as Ford would have done. I had been asked before if those were wood spokes and from that moment on, there would be no doubt from people that they were wood! Come that spring, I was ready for another season, punctuated by another trip to Pine Bluffs.

T-Curse of Pine Bluffs – 2024

"Here we go again." I thought as I put the event on my calendar. This time, there was no tour planned. I made no plans with anyone. I figured I needed to do this one without potentially impacting someone else. If I succeeded or succumbed to disaster, yet again, it would be only me facing the inconvenience.

Early in the season, I noticed extra noise coming from the rear end as well as from inside the engine. Jim was willing to look over my car, but he no longer had a trailer. My friend JJ did though, and he helped haul my car down to Jim to look over the engine noise.

Once we got Patience down to Jim's shop, he pulled out his mechanic's stethoscope. If you've never seen one of those in action, hop online and look them up! I ended up buying one myself after using Jim's. There was a slight knock coming from the general area of the valves. We opened it up and checked the clearances, all within spec! We did end up finding soot accumulation around the exhaust manifold, indicating a small leak. I bought some new copper manifold crush-style gasket rings, and we got everything buttoned back up. The knocking sound was much quieter, but still there. As I have aluminum pistons, the slight noise was attributed to minor piston slap resulting from likely intentionally loose pistons, intended to accommodate the thermal expansion of the aluminum inside of the cast iron engine. Or perhaps it was some wrist pin knock, no one really knew! I was told the noise wasn't too serious. Keep an eye on it, let her warm up before putting a load on the engine, and most importantly, drive the car! Enjoy the car! Share the history!

Once loaded onto the trailer, Jim had noticed that the muffler had fallen apart. The rear end noise was a result of a blown muffler. At some point, I must have had a minor backfire that blew loose the baffles. "Fix that muffler!" Jim declared as we loaded up to head back to Cheyenne. Once the car got home, the following weekend, I took off the muffler. It was about the dirtiest repair I had undertaken. So much carbon soot fell out everywhere. I spent much of the following weekend just cleaning up soot! Afterwards, I repositioned the baffles and tightened down the bolt holding it all together. The muffler was fixed! Rear end noise was normal again. Patience was ready for the rest of the season and hopefully, a trip to Pine Bluffs.

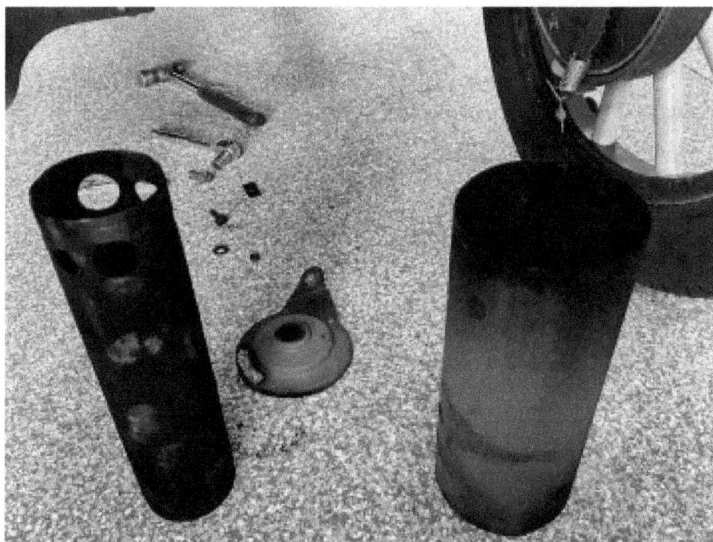

The 2024 driving season went by quite well. I wasn't doing anything too crazy that year. I went to numerous parades, car shows, cars and coffee events and club meetings. Patience was having a really good year! As we got closer to August, and another Trail Days parade in Pine Bluffs, one of the Oak Spokes members wanted to come along. This year Bob wanted to go with me. He was the Oak Spokes President the year I joined. He wanted to take his Model A. I was apprehensive about traveling with someone in the event Patience had another issue. I really wasn't worried about my safety; I just didn't want the embarrassment of causing someone else a delay in their plans. I told Bob I would meet him there rather than convoy over with him. He agreed and we made plans to do the parade and car show afterwards. I had some friends who wanted to ride in the parade also, I told them I'd meet them there for the same reasons mentioned earlier, plus they had young children who wanted to ride with me too.

The night before the drive and parade was marked like many nights on the eve of a parade or car show. I did my safety checks, topped off fluids, air pressure checks, and looked for leaks. All systems go! That following morning, I got up early and let Patience warm up well before starting off. The new radiator did such a great job that it took a lot longer to warm up to operating temperature than the old radiator did. After a good 15 or 20 minutes of warming up, I drove over to the gas station, topped off, and then set off down the interstate access road destined for some sort of day.

I got to Pine Bluffs just in time to get into the line ahead of the start of the parade. The only issue was, I could not find a way over the parade route to get to the line. I was starting to panic a little until I managed to find someone willing to open the barricade to let me shoot over to the staging area. I spotted Bob and pulled up adjacent to him in line. Bob was chatting away with some of the others in the parade who were interested in his very nicely restored Model A. I saw my friends walking up to me.

I prepared my friends for the quick, 25-minute parade that was to follow. Bob told me to pull ahead of his car since mine was oldest and Oak Spokes tradition is to line up by the year of the car, oldest to newest. There were no politicians this year that I could see, but lots of the usual local folks who were excited to celebrate their town. It made me happy. Suddenly, the line started to move, so Bob and I fired up our cars and prepared to start down the parade route. My friends in the back seat were happily throwing candy to all of the kids as we made our way down main street. I was feeling relieved, happy, and grateful to be able to drive successfully down the main street. Like my first year, we ran out of candy about halfway down the street, but there were still others throwing candy around us and the kids didn't seem to notice.

After the parade, I returned my passengers to their car at the start of the parade route as they were going to feed their children and meet me and Bob at the car show. I drove down to the car show and parked next to Bob. I hopped out and Bob and I walked up to the saloon's entrance to formally register for the car show. Lots and lots of other cars started filing into the dirt parking lot. The nearby closed street ended up hosting numerous vehicles due to the lack of space. I felt surprised to see how successful the event was this year. I had no idea where they all came from though, as most of these vehicles were not in the parade.

Bob and I walked inside the saloon and got a table. My friend and his wife showed up with their kids – despite the saloon hosting the event, it was made to be family friendly. After a while, my wife and son came as well. We all talked and had a great time for a couple of hours before my friends and family went home. Bob and I remained. We had about an hour before the event ended, so we ran to get a quick bite and then came back to see who won the various categories. Bob and I won nothing that year; however, the saloon's proprietor told us that if we gave him a heads up, in 2025, he would make some more categories for our older, more vintage vehicles. He also told us that the local newspaper wanted to talk to us before we set off! After a quick chat with the local news reporter on the history of our cars, he wanted a photograph of a few of the cars from the show all lined up, oldest to newest, to highlight the event in the newspaper. After lining up, he snapped his pictures, and we took some photos with our phones. Even though we didn't win, being in the newspaper was pretty neat.

I told Bob I had some other things in town I wanted to check out before I left for Cheyenne. We said our goodbyes, and he set off. I left the saloon to head up to the distillery. I wanted a bottle of their limited release for Trail Days. I told my friend I would bring him back a bottle, too. Upon arriving at the distillery, there was maybe one or two people there. Everyone else was still in the main part of town. I picked up two bottles (numbers 8 and 9 of the limited release), and then I travelled briefly east to the Wyoming/Nebraska state line. The "Our Lady of Peace Shrine" was something I wanted to see with Patience. I pulled up into the dirt parking lot and walked around for about half an hour and took some pictures of Patience at the shrine.

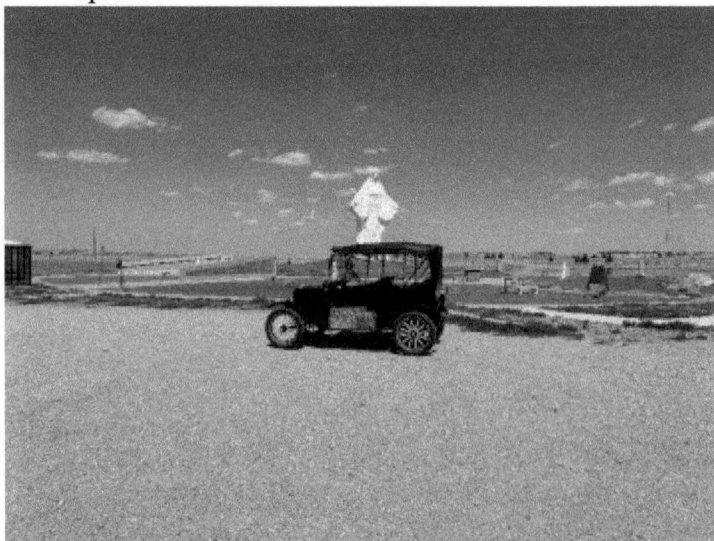

Above: the largest Marian shrine in the USA (30 feet tall) she seems surprised I was able to make the trip!

From the shrine, I had one last landmark I wanted to see. Smack on the state line are the remnants of a now dilapidated gas station. Once one of the busiest in the area until Interstate 80 was completed in this area in the late 1960s, it now sits abandoned. I really wanted to get some pictures of it. I parked along the roadside and took dozens of photos at different angles to try and get the perfect shot. Since I was not able to get right up to the old filling station, my pictures were not perfect, but I was still glad to be there.

After grabbing many photographs at the state line, I decided it was time to hurry home while there was still daylight, especially in the event disaster were to strike. I drove into Nebraska for a couple of miles, just to say I did, then turned around and went back towards Pine Bluffs to gas up and head home to Cheyenne.

The drive home was both relaxing and tense. "What could go wrong?" I kept asking myself. I made sure not to push Patience too hard on the open stretch of road. Taking my time and having "patience", I made my usual stop at the midway point to gas up and do a quick once over – I saw nothing wrong; no signs of overheating, nothing falling off the car, oil still leaking out of the appropriate places. I started the final push home. After another thankfully uneventful 20 or so minutes, I was pulling into my garage! Was the curse finally broken? I was ecstatic! Once parked safely in my garage, I gave another quick once over. "Nothing broken!" I exclaimed. "Wait.... wait a minute..." I muttered as I honed in on my spare tire in its carrier...I always check the spare when I check the other tires to make sure they are all at 61 PSI, but my spare was clearly no longer at 61 PSI. At the beginning of the day, all five tires were at pressure. Somehow, someway, the valve stem on the spare tire burst! I started chuckling, then laughing. The absurdity of the moment was hilarious for me. Given the very minor nuisance this presented in comparison to every other trip I made in Patience to Pine Bluffs, I considered the day an overall success.

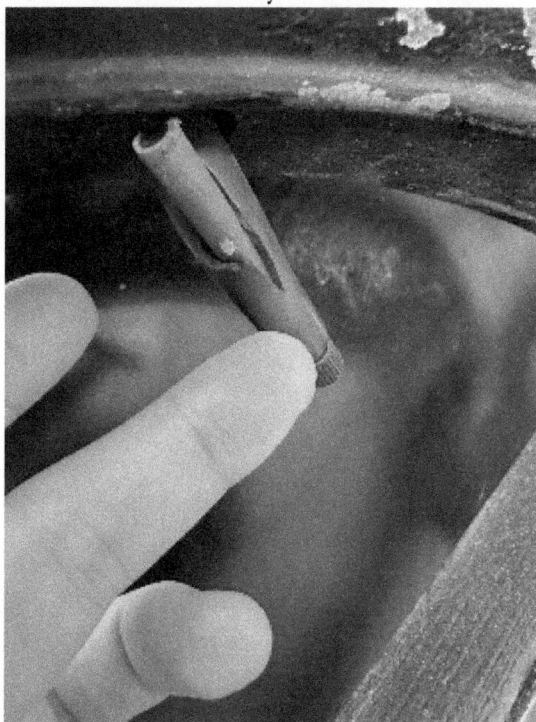

Above: Is this the last gasps of the Curse of Pine Bluffs? I sure hope so! Time will tell.

The AdvenTures ConTinue

A s I write this, Patience and I prepare for another year of touring, traveling, and adventure. I have tentative plans and goals for trips and more adventures for at least the next two summers. Things that I may write about when it makes sense for me to do so. Patience continues to teach me things. I have made a number of other various repairs, tweaks and adjustments that I could not address earlier because they just happen through due course of owning a 100-year-old vehicle. Besides the mechanical, a lot of what Patience has taught me are things not related to the tangible aspects of a Model T. I have learned that the two most important aspects of T-raveling are the people and the history.

Many of us can attest that we are not 'owners' of vintage cars like a Model T, but rather 'stewards' of them and the history they carry and represent. These cars are survivors and have seen, and been part of, a chain of events and history that extends back to the beginnings of automotive history, road trips, and an interconnected nation of states in a very true sense. The Model T triggered the development of modern roads and allowed for a mode of travel that just was not as easy or commonplace prior to its creation. The fact that these cars still exist in such large numbers today is testament not only to their importance in history, but also to their durability.

Despite my many mechanical issues, these are very, very durable vehicles. I do not anticipate anything that I have had to fix or repair to fail again in my lifetime. The roads of today are nothing at all in comparison to yesteryear and the Model T can really excel as a daily driver today, within reason. These vehicles obviously cannot handle interstate travel but can and should be driven within a town or along access roads to neighboring towns, as much as possible! These are simple machines that were designed to be maintained and repaired by their operator. I am of the honest opinion that these stalwart machines of yesterday can be easily driven and maintained by anyone, after a bit of a learning curve. Don't feel overwhelmed by the levers and pedals, they really are not that bad after a couple weeks of dedicated practice. Just remember, stomp those pedals! Don't let them slip!

The other aspect to this are the people. I have met some of the best human beings as a result of this hobby. The friends and acquaintances I have made as a result of membership in the clubs has caused real and meaningful changes in my life. These folks who drive vintage automobiles, not only the Model T, but everything before and after, are genuine and salt of the earth. They have a real understanding of what life is all about. Being in the parades, going to parks, driving to work, driving through my neighborhood and around town has connected me with some interesting people outside of the car community. With my car acting as a social lubricator, I have met people who have interesting histories of their own and often fall into the niches and obscure corners of life that you just don't readily connect with outside of the social lubrication a Model T provides.

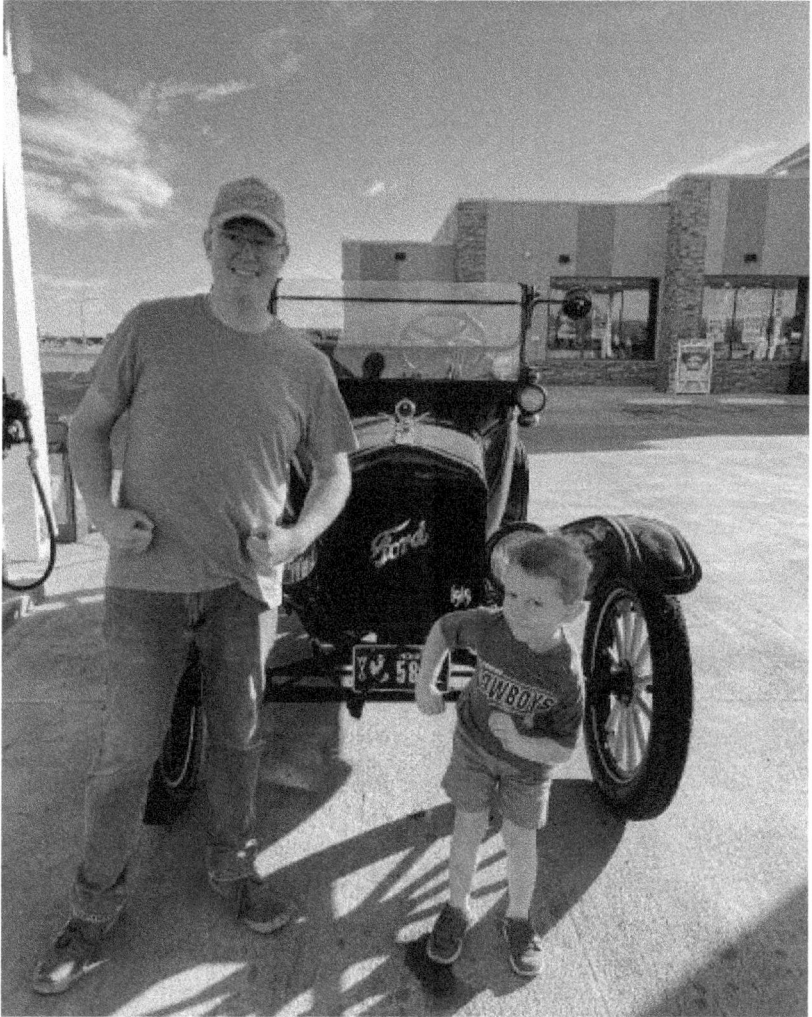

While I do not like to do a lot of traveling, I do consider myself to be a T-raveler. Patience has tested me on many occasions. The experiences, both good and bad, have helped me to become as durable in character and spirit as the steel of my car. We both understand what difficulties we have faced and survived over the years. Each drive and each adventure are greeted with open arms, eyes, and a come what may attitude.

Until next time!

See you down the road!

About the Author

Jason Bogstie has owned a Ford Model T since 2021. He drives his 1919 Touring, lovingly named 'Patience', as frequently as he can. Jason presently resides in Cheyenne, Wyoming, with his wife (Emily) and son (Oliver). In 2025, Jason was elected to join the Board of Directors for the Model T Ford Club of America (MTFCA). As of 2025, Jason is also the current President of the Oak Spokes chapter of the Antique Automobile Club of America (AACA) and the President of the High Plains Region of the AACA. His other interests include amateur radio (NW7N), cigars, and scotch.

www.ingramcontent.com/pod-product-compliance
Lightning Source LLC
LaVergne TN
LVHW041231080426
835508LV00011B/1161